SNAP
SHOT™

Art director Roger Priddy
Editor Mary Ling
Assistant designer
Joanna Pocock

SNAPSHOT™
is an imprint of Covent Garden Books.
232 Madison Avenue,
New York, New York 10016

Copyright © 1994 Covent Garden
Books Limited, London.

Photography copyright © 1991
Jerry Young.
Photography by Dave King, Jane Burton,
Kim Taylor, Steve Shott and Frank Greenaway.
2 4 6 8 10 9 7 5 3 1

Color reproduction by Colourscan
Printed in U.S.A.

WILD ANIMALS

Contents

Brown bear

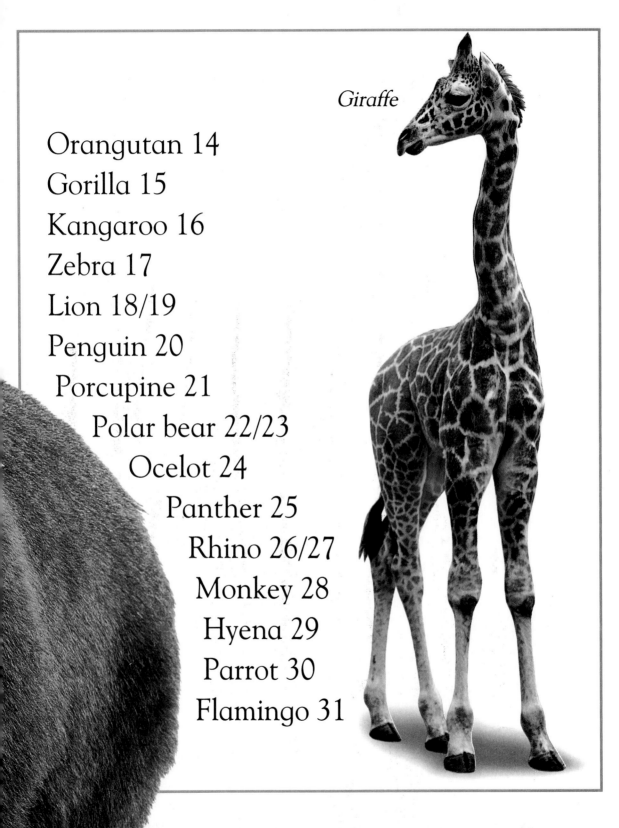

Giraffe

What do pandas munch?

Pandas nibble all day on a tasty grass called bamboo.

Does a tiger need stripes?

A tiger's striped coat
helps it hunt in the grass
without being seen.

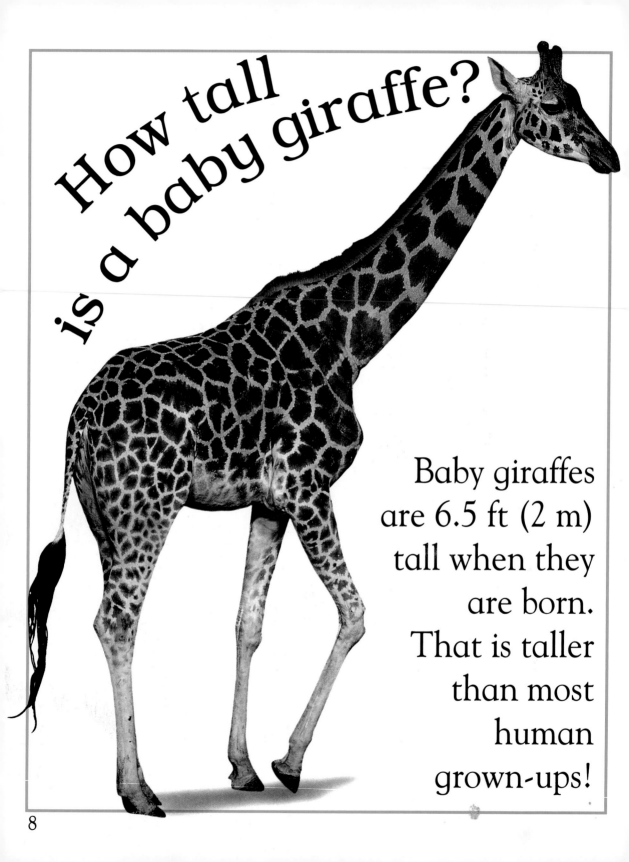

How tall is a baby giraffe?

Baby giraffes are 6.5 ft (2 m) tall when they are born. That is taller than most human grown-ups!

What do trunks do?

An elephant uses its amazing trunk to breathe, carry food, or even take a cooling shower.

What do bears do in winter?

Brown bears sleep all winter.
They dig a den in the ground and
sleep, warm and dry, until spring.

What's in a camel's hump?

Camels keep fat in their humps – like a lunch box, for energy on long walks.

Does a 'roo need a tail?

Kangaroos use their tails as props to sit on when they feel like taking a rest.

Smart suit!

Zebras like
to groom one another
to keep their striped suits clean!

How loud is a lion's roar?

A lion roars very loudly to protect his pride and scare away other cats. His mighty meow means, "Beware, I'm angry!"

Can I fly?

A penguin cannot fly.
It uses its flippers
for swimming.
On land, it
hops along
or slides
on its
belly.

What are my quills for?

Porcupines are covered in sharp spikes, called quills. If attacked, it may reverse and give the enemy a prickly surprise!

Do polar bears get cold?

This polar bear has a layer of fat under its thick fur that keeps it warm in cold blizzards.

Can you spot me?

An ocelot's spotted coat helps it hide in the undergrowth when it is hunting.

Night hunter!

Panthers hunt at night. Their eyes are six times stronger than human eyes.

What is a rhino's

A rhinocerous has very thick skin that protects it against insect stings, prickly bushes, or even a lion's sharp teeth.

armor made of ?

Who's a clever monkey?

For its
tiny size,
this squirrel
monkey has
a very large brain.

What's so funny?

The hyena
doesn't howl or roar. It
makes a noise that sounds like a laugh.

What a show-off!

Many parrots
like to show off
their bright colors
to attract mates.

Which way is up?

Flamingos dip their strange bills upside down into water and sift the mud, looking for juicy worms and insects.